Adventure Story Bible
Book 14

Micah, Joel & Jonah

Written by Anne de Graaf

Illustrated by José Pérez Montero

Bible Society

JONAH AND THE BIG FISH

Runaway from God

Jonah 1:1-3

There once was a man called Jonah. He was one of God's people, the Israelites. He came from Galilee, the same area Jesus would later come from.

One day God said to Jonah, "I want you to go to the city of Nineveh. Tell them they are living such wicked lives, I will have to punish them."

Jonah did not like Nineveh. It was the capital of the great Assyrian empire. The people of Nineveh were enemies of God's people.

But God was willing to forgive the Ninevites if they would only change their ways. The Ninevites were the cruelest people in the world at that time. If God could forgive them, He could forgive anybody.

Jonah did not like this. "Why should God care about them?" he wondered. So Jonah did a foolish thing. He ignored God. He turned his back on God and ran away from Nineveh, rather than toward it. That way, the Ninevites would not be warned about how angry God was with them. Jonah wanted the Ninevites to be destroyed.

But Jonah had made a mistake. There is no place where people can hide from God. He is everywhere and knows everything.

Jonah tried to go to Tarshish, a city in Spain, far away from the Assyrians. Tarshish was in the opposite direction of Nineveh. He went down to the harbor, a place called Joppa. That is where the city of Tel-Aviv now stands.

In Joppa, Jonah wandered up and down the docks. He was looking for a ship which would take him clear to the other side of the world. Jonah found one headed for Tarshish. That was far enough.

He made sure he put as much distance between himself and Nineveh as possible. Once the ship set sail, Jonah breathed a sigh of relief. "Now those evil Ninevites will get what they deserve," he thought to himself.

Storm at Sea

Jonah 1:4-16

Once on board, Jonah soon fell asleep. He thought he could relax because he had run away from God. He was wrong.

The Lord threw a great wind at the sea. A terrible storm shook the waves and the ship was thrown first this way, then that. The sailors on Jonah's boat could tell this was an unusually bad storm. "There must be some reason why this is happening. Someone on the ship must have made his god angry," they yelled at each other over the wind.

So each sailor prayed to his own god, begging to be saved. Nothing happened. The wind howled louder, the waves reared higher and higher over the boat.

5

The captain ordered all the cargo to be thrown overboard. But the ship still threatened to sink. Finally the captain went below deck and woke Jonah up. "How can you be sleeping through a storm like this?" he asked. "You should be praying to your God. Maybe He will be able to save us from this storm."

The men on board tried to find out whose fault it was that they were being punished with such a horrible storm. They went to Jonah.

"Tell us now! Why has this happened? Who are you and where do you come from?" they yelled over the wind. "Who are your people?"

Jonah said, "I am a Jew. My people believe in the Lord God of heaven. He made the sea and dry land."

The men became very frightened. They had heard about this Lord God of Israel before. They gasped, "How could you do this?" They knew Jonah was trying to run away from God. They also knew that was impossible. God sees everything.

"It is your God who is punishing us. Now tell us, how do we stop this storm?"

Jonah said, "If you throw me overboard, the storm will go away. I know it's my fault that the Lord has done this to you."

At first they were not willing to throw Jonah into the sea. The sailors rowed and rowed with all their strength, hoping they could still save the ship. After several hours of this, though, they gave up. They had tried their best to save Jonah, but the sea just grew more and more wild.

The sailors prayed to Jonah's God, "Oh, Lord. Please don't kill us with this storm. We haven't done anything wrong. Only this man has." They had no choice. They picked up Jonah and threw him into the raging sea.

Suddenly, the wind stopped howling and the waves died down. "Oh no!" the sailors cried. "The God of Jonah really did send the storm!" The men were very afraid. They offered sacrifices to God and promised to believe in Him.

The Big Fish

Jonah 1:17-2:10

After the sailors threw him overboard, Jonah felt himself sinking deeper and deeper into the sea. He closed his eyes and held his breath, waiting until he would start floating up toward the top again. But that did not happen.

Instead he felt something cold and slimy bump up against him. He opened his eyes and would have screamed with fright if he had not been underwater. A giant fish was swimming around and around him!

Before Jonah had time to even think about how to get away, the giant fish opened its mouth wide and "Swoosh!" Jonah was swept into its mouth and swallowed into the stomach of the fish!

Because the fish was so large, Jonah found he could stand up inside and breathe again. It was very dark and smelled sour.

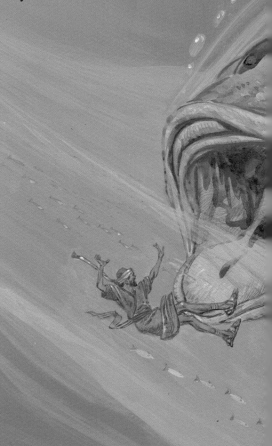

It was not by chance that the fish had swallowed Jonah. God had chosen this fish to teach Jonah that no matter where he went, he could never run away from God. God wanted Jonah to do what He had been told and go to Nineveh with the Lord's message.

For three days and three nights Jonah prayed to God from inside the giant fish. Slowly, as Jonah prayed in that dark, smelly place, he learned that God could take care of him, even when he sat inside the belly of a fish. Jonah did not grow angry at God. Instead, he said he was sorry, and thanked the Lord for not forgetting him.

After three days and three nights, the Lord made the fish spit Jonah out of its stomach. With a great wet rush, Jonah held his breath again as he swirled around inside the fish's mouth. The next thing he knew, he was lying on a dry beach, looking up at the sunshine.

Jonah Changes His Mind

Jonah 3:1-10

For a second time the Lord told Jonah, "Go on now. Go to Nineveh and tell them whatever message I give you."

This time Jonah did as he was told. Nineveh was a gigantic city, people's homes spread out for miles around. Jonah started walking from one end to the other. It took him three days to walk around the city. Day after day he walked up and down streets and in between houses.

All day long he called out the message God had given him. "In forty days Nineveh will be destroyed!" He told the people of Nineveh God would wipe their city off the face of the earth.

The people of Nineveh heard Jonah and were shocked. This was terrible news! They listened to God's warnings. They believed in God. They took off their rich clothes and wore plain, old clothing, made of sackcloth. They stopped eating and spent their days praying. Everyone from the poorest beggar to the richest farmer asked God to forgive them for living such evil lives.

Even the king of Nineveh laid aside his robe and put on the sackcloth clothes. He ordered everybody to do the same. "Do not let man, beast, herd, or flock taste a thing.… "

When God saw how all the people were sorry and wanted to change, He forgave them. They were not His own people, yet they had listened when God sent them the prophet Jonah. God had mercy and chose not to destroy the people of Nineveh.

God Is Good

Jonah 4:1-11

When God decided to let the people of Nineveh live, Jonah was not very happy. He prayed to the Lord, "Lord, I knew You would do this. I knew You were a kind, loving God, always ready to forgive people and give them another chance. Now You've saved Nineveh, that awful city and all those evil people! It just isn't fair!"

Jonah wanted the Ninevites to die. He thought he made more sense than God. Why did God care about the Ninevites, anyway? Jonah thought the Lord was God of the Jews, not anybody else. But God had decided to forgive the Ninevites. This made Jonah very, very angry.

The Lord said, "Jonah, what is the matter? Why are you so upset?"

Jonah went off to a place east of the city to sulk. That day, as Jonah sat in the hot sun, waiting and watching. God caused a plant to grow so that it shaded Jonah from the sunlight. Thanks to the plant, he could look out over the city without becoming too hot. This plant was the only good thing in Jonah's life.

But God had a worm attack the plant and by sunrise the next day, it had withered. God called the hot east wind to blow and the sun to beat down on Jonah's head. That day he became faint and begged with all his might, "Please Lord, I am furious at this plant. Even it has failed me. Please put me out of my suffering."

God asked Jonah, "Why should you be angry at the plant?"

Jonah said, "Of course I have good reason to be angry! I want that plant back."

Then the Lord said, "You are angry because this plant died. You wanted it to live, even though you did not plant it. It came up one night and died the next. Now why shouldn't I care in the same way, if not more, for the over hundred thousand people in Nineveh? They did not know until you told them that what they were doing was so wrong.

"This was the reason I sent you to them. They needed to learn that what they thought was normal living, was really very bad. They had been believing in gods which just made them afraid. Now, through you, they have met Me. Once they understood, they said they were sorry."

God wanted Jonah to see that He loved people in Nineveh, just as Jonah had come to like the plant which had given him shade. Jonah wanted the plant to live, yet he had not made it grow. How much more God must have cared for the Ninevites, who were men and women and children that God had created and loved. That is why He did not destroy them.

Throughout it all, God taught the prophet Jonah a whale of a lesson.

THE PROPHET HOSEA
A Broken Marriage

Hosea 1:1-3:5

The prophet Hosea preached to the kingdom of Israel. He lived during a terrible time, just before Samaria fell to Assyria. God's people were choosing again and again to forget about God. They worshiped other gods and broke God's laws. God wanted them to know they should stop acting like the tribes around them and be His special people again. He very much wanted the Israelites to come back to Him. He wanted to love and forgive them, but the choice was theirs.

The prophet Hosea helped show the people just how badly they had hurt God. He did this by obeying God when God told Hosea to marry

a prostitute. This was a bad woman named Gomer. Gomer hurt Hosea in the same ways that Israel hurt God. She broke his heart.

Then God used Hosea's family to teach the people what they were doing to Him. Even Gomer's children were named after the warnings God wanted His people to hear.

Gomer's first child was named Jezreel. This meant "He Scatters" or "He Sows." The Lord wanted His people to know He is the One who makes the sun shine and rain fall so crops can grow. Many of His people thought some other god was in charge of that. God wanted His people to know that if they did not stop worshiping other gods, they would be taken prisoner by the Assyrians.

Gomer's second child was a little girl named Lo-ruhamah. This meant "I Do Not Love Her." God wanted very much to love His people, if only they would let Him.

Gomer's third child was called Lo-ammi, which meant "Not My People." If only they would turn from their bad living, God could say again, "You are My people!"

Again and again, Gomer ran away from Hosea. No matter how many other men she chased after, though, Hosea always brought her home. "Let's start over," he would say lovingly. It was enough for Hosea that he had his wife back again. Hosea loved Gomer. But Gomer kept falling into the same hurtful ways of living.

Once, she even became another man's slave. Hosea had to buy her back. Gomer had run away and Hosea did not see her again for many years. One day, he happened to see some slaves for sale. One of them, a woman who looked thin and ugly, was his very own wife!

"Gomer!" he called to her, but she looked away. Once again Hosea loved and forgave her, only wanting to start over. So he bought Gomer for half the usual price.

"Let's try and start over. I do love you, can't that be enough?" he asked her. Gomer said nothing. She had shut out Hosea's love.

In the same way, God's people had shut out His love.

Evil Ways of Life

Hosea 4:1-14:9

During the horrible years before the Assyrians took Samaria, the prophet Hosea often tried to teach the people. "Listen! Hear what the Lord has to say!" But nobody listened. People did not care. It was more fun to follow the gods of the other tribes. That way they could do whatever they pleased.

There was swearing, lying, murder, stealing and violence. Husbands and wives forgot who they were married to. Nobody took care of the children anymore. God warned that because the people no longer taught their children about His laws, He would no longer take care of them.

The leaders and priests should have known better. They had misled the people. The false gods which Israel and Judah worshiped could not help them when they were in trouble.

God told them through Hosea, "Be kind and good to each other. That is worth much more than all your empty words and broken promises."

The people only cared about their rich things. Money and power were more important than family and friends. They trusted their riches.

Hosea said, "Wise people would know the ways of the Lord were right. Good people would want to walk in those ways. The rest of you will stumble and fall!"

If they did not change soon, God would use the Assyrians to strip them of their homes and families. They would spend the rest of their lives as slaves and be left with nothing.

THE PROPHET JOEL

Locusts and Hope

Joel 1:1-20

Joel was another prophet used by God to warn the people. In his time, a huge swarm of locust insects attacked Jerusalem. Millions of the little flying creatures flew in a cloud over the city. When they landed, they crawled into everything, eating every green and growing thing they could find.

These insects were everywhere, in people's hair and mouths, and in their ears. No matter if you stayed inside and locked all the doors, you could still hear the hum of thousands of locusts eating, eating, eating anything they could find. The hum was more like the roar of a lion when he attacks. But locusts are worse than lions, added together they have more teeth.

The locusts ate all the crops, so there were no grapes to make wine. There was no grain to make flour for bread and no fruit or vegetables. The people did not even have enough to offer back to God in thanks for the harvest. They needed every bit of food to keep from starving to death. It was a terrible, terrible time for the people of Jerusalem.

And yet, God promised the people through Joel, "Call Me your God again and I will pay you back for the years the locusts have eaten. They were My great army. Come back to Me and I will protect you. You will have plenty to eat, until you are full. Just know that I am the Lord your God."

Making It Right

Joel 2:1-3:21

Joel said God had used the locusts to show that the people should believe in Him, not any of the fake gods. Joel asked all the people to stop whatever they were doing and have a day of prayer.

God had tried to teach His people an important lesson about how He would someday judge them. They said they were sorry and prayed, hoping for the forgiveness God was only too glad to give.

Now they knew just how bad they had been to turn away from God. They saw in the swarm of locusts how it would be when God did judge them and they trembled with fear.

God was great and they were afraid. Why, God could even tell the insects what to do! Joel warned them to remember, no matter how it might seem like they could get away with living bad lives, everyone must someday pay for all the wrong things they had done.

But the news Joel had for the people was not all bad. If the nation of God's people would turn to Him, God promised to forgive them. He even promised to make the people richer than they were before the locusts came.

This was a promise that seemed almost too good to be true. God said through Joel, "You will have plenty to eat, until you are full. When you come back to Me, when you know that I am the Lord your God, you will never be shamed." How could the people ever let such a chance pass them by? And yet many would do just that.

MORE KINGS

Proud Uzziah

2 Kings 15:1-7; 2 Chronicles 26:1-23

At this time there lived a king of Judah named Uzziah. Uzziah became king when he was sixteen years old. He began his rule teaching the people to follow God's Law. Uzziah ruled for fifty-two years.

He was a strong king who defeated the Philistines and Arabs. He even managed to defeat the Ammonites. But because Uzziah grew to become a proud king, he died a sick and unhappy man.

In the beginning, Uzziah tried to do whatever God asked of him. In return, God blessed him and helped Uzziah win back the kingdom of Judah as far south as the Red Sea.

Uzziah loved the land. He liked nothing better than to see his people working in the fields and the soil rich with harvest. To help the farmers, he repaired the wells, protected the people's cattle and had many workers plowing fields and taking care of the crops.

His army was famous. People from as far away as Egypt had heard about Uzziah's army. He built great towers to protect Jerusalem. Uzziah even built war machines which shot missiles of arrows and big stones.

After he became strong, though, Uzziah's pride in himself made him weak. He chose to forget that it was the Lord who had made him strong and defeated his enemies.

Uzziah thought to himself, "I am so great, I can make myself into a priest of God." This was wrong since only God could choose His priests. These had to be men from the family of Aaron, Moses' brother.

To show Uzziah how wrong he was, God struck him down with leprosy. The skin on Uzziah's forehead grew white and flaky. This happened even as the priests in the temple were warning him to stop lighting the incense. He was a very sick man. As a leper, he could never again enter the temple to worship.

Uzziah had to spend the rest of his life living alone in a house away from all the other people. He died unhappy. If he had been satisfied with being king, the Lord would have continued blessing him. But Uzziah had made the mistake of wanting more.

God Calls Isaiah

Isaiah 6:1-13

While the prophet Hosea was warning the people of Israel to stop loving themselves more than God, the prophet Isaiah was saying the same to the people of Judah.

One day, when Isaiah was in Jerusalem, he had a special vision. God let Isaiah see into heaven. Isaiah said he saw "the Lord sitting on a throne. His robe filled the temple."

In the vision, Isaiah cried out, "Oh no! I will be destroyed. I am not pure. I've said so many bad things in my life. And I live around bad people. Yet my eyes have seen the King, the Lord. He is so perfect, and I am nothing!"

But the Lord let Isaiah know that He forgave him. He made Isaiah into a messenger of God.

Isaiah said, "I heard a Voice say, 'Who will go for Us?'

I said, 'Send me!'"

The Lord told Isaiah to try and help the people to listen, look, see and hear all that God wanted to show them. He warned that someday many of them would be taken prisoner because they were so stubborn. Some would come back to start over again, though.

Isaiah never forgot what he saw that day. He had come very close to God. All his sin was taken away.

For the rest of his life, Isaiah would speak God's words to His people. Over and over again he told them about God's love, how much He wanted to be close to His people, if only they would let Him.

Israel's Bad Kings

2 Kings 15:8-31

During the twenty-one years between 753 B.C. and 732 B.C., Israel had six kings. That four of these kings were killed by the men who became king in their places, just shows how wicked the kingdom of Israel was at that time. People would do anything to get more power.

One after another, bad kings took the throne. They ruled from Samaria, the head city of Israel. The first one was a king called Zechariah. He was the son of Jeroboam and ruled for only six months. Zechariah was just as evil as some of the kings of Israel before him. He led the people away from God.

A man named Shallum plotted against Zechariah. He killed him in front of the people and made himself king. But this man only lasted as king for one month. He, too, was very evil.

Then Menahem went to Samaria from his hometown Tirzah. He struck Shallum dead and made himself king instead. But the people of Tiphsah knew he was no king. So they told him he should get off the throne. Menahem did not like this. He sent an army to Tiphsah and hurt the people there very badly.

Menahem ruled as king over Israel for ten years. God watched sadly as Menahem made the people of Israel worship other gods. When the king of Assyria attacked Israel, Menahem paid him a great deal of silver so that he would not attack. The Assyrians went back home, but they would soon return.

When Menahem died, his son Pekahiah became king in his place. He reigned two years, then one of his officers, a man named Pekah, did something horrible. He plotted against the king and killed him right inside the palace.

Pekah ruled for twenty years, but he was no better than the kings who had gone before him. While Pekah was king, the Assyrian king came back. This time he attacked Israel over and over again. The Assyrians captured one city after another. They carried the people away to Assyria, just as the prophets had warned would happen. But they had not captured Samaria, where the king lived.

Pekah was killed by Hoshea, who became king in his place. Hoshea would be the last king of Israel. It would not be long before Assyria would defeat all of Israel and nothing would be left of that half of the kingdom of God's people.

Isaiah Speaks God's Message

Isaiah 1:1-5:30

During this dark and troubled time, Isaiah walked up and down the land. Over and over again he warned the people of Judah and Jerusalem that God would allow the enemy Assyrians to capture them and make them slaves if they did not stop living such evil lives.

The people had turned their backs on God. They no longer cared if they lived good lives or bad. They hurt poor people, did not help widows and ignored orphans. All they wanted was for themselves. The leaders were all liars and robbers. They would do anything for money.

The evil priests and kings had taught the people not to follow God's Law anymore. The people's hearts were far from Him. Nobody even tried to be kind. They were all too selfish.

Any prayers the people said, were fake and done just to impress their friends. The people said one thing and did another. The rich became richer and the poor suffered even more.

Isaiah said that someday they would have to pay for all the wrong things they had done. "Woe to the wicked!" Isaiah called out.

Isaiah sang a song which described a vineyard. It was really about how God saw His people. "There once was a vineyard which was planted in good soil. All the stones were taken away. The best vines were used. The plants were carefully tended, but they did not produce good grapes. No matter how well the workers searched, they could find only a few sour grapes."

Isaiah told them God would stop taking care of Israel, His worthless vineyard. He had given them every chance to become good people, but they had all turned out bad.

Isaiah warned that the people were heading for terrible times. Their own selfishness would make them easy victims for the Assyrian armies. The leaders of God's people, in particular, had to start taking better care of the poor. Every time they hurt people who were less well off than themselves, God saw and felt the pain.

King Jotham

2 Kings 15:32-38; 2 Chronicles 27:1-9

At the same time that Israel was ruled by the six bad kings, Judah had a good king. This was the son of Uzziah, who had thought he was so great, he could become a priest in the temple of God. The Lord had punished Uzziah for his pride and made him sick with leprosy.

Uzziah's son was a man named Jotham. He became king when he was twenty-five years old and he ruled for sixteen years. Jotham was a good king because he tried to do what the Lord wanted. In this way he was like his father. But he did not try and be a priest in God's temple. So in that way he was better than Uzziah.

Jotham built many forts and towers. He defeated the Ammonites, and protected the people from Aram and Israel.

Every day Jotham prayed to God, "Please help me to lead the people. Show me what You want me to do. I trust You, Lord." Because of this, God blessed Jotham and made him a strong king with mighty armies.

King Jotham of Judah tried to bring the people back to following God's laws, but they would not listen. The king tore down most of the places for worshiping false gods and left only a few on top of the hills and mountains. But still, the people chose to turn their backs on God.

Ahaz the Very Bad King

2 Kings 16:1-20; 2 Chronicles 28:1-27

The son of King Jotham was a man called Ahaz. Ahaz became king of Judah when he was twenty years old. Like his father, he ruled for sixteen years in Jerusalem. But that was the only thing he had in common with the good King Jotham. King Ahaz was very, very bad, just as bad as the kings of Israel at that time.

He set up places to worship the false gods on every hill and under every tall tree. He worshiped the Lord together with other gods. This made the Lord very, very sad. Now both Israel and Judah had forgotten about how much God wanted to love them.

The kings of Israel and Aram attacked Jerusalem. They killed many thousands of people and took two hundred thousand women and children prisoner. King Ahaz was also taken prisoner. They marched the people to Samaria and were going to make them into slaves.

A prophet for the Lord named Oded was there. He told the Israelites God was angry at Judah.

"But you people from Israel have also done wrong things against the Lord your God, haven't you?" Yes, Israel was just as guilty as Judah.

There were some leaders that day who heard the prophet. "We do not want God to punish us," they thought. So they ordered that the prisoners, including King Ahaz, should be fed and clothed, then led back to Jericho where they could rest before going on home.

But King Ahaz did not learn his lesson from this. Even though his enemies had shown him kindness, he was not at all thankful to the Lord. He should have seen his new freedom as a chance to start over. Instead, he became even worse, worshiping any god he could find, except the one true God.

Later, Israel and Aram attacked Jerusalem again. But they did not manage to defeat the city. Day after day, week after week, Ahaz held out against the two armies.

God Warns King Ahaz

Isaiah 7:1-9

Because King Ahaz did not do what God asked, his kingdom of Judah was attacked, not by one army, but two! Both Aram and Israel tried to capture Judah. Jerusalem was surrounded by soldiers from the two enemy armies.

King Ahaz did not go to the temple to pray to God. He prayed to his false god, instead, just like the rest of the people in Jerusalem. But just when it looked as though Jerusalem would be captured, the prophet Isaiah went to King Ahaz. "It will be all right. Be calm! Don't be frightened. God says these two armies are nothing. They think they will capture Jerusalem, but it will never happen. You must choose to trust in God, though, and stop praying to these false gods. Otherwise there is no way you can last."

Ahaz had a choice. He could trust God to take care of Jerusalem and the people living there. Or he could choose not to believe in God. He chose not to trust God. Instead, he made a deal with another king, the king of Assyria who was also an enemy of Israel.

Ahaz paid the king of Assyria all the silver and gold he could find inside God's temple, the one Solomon had built. The Assyrians helped Ahaz then, and chased off the armies of Aram and Israel. They captured their kings and put them to death.

Ahaz began to worship the false gods of Assyria. Because of this, though, the temple of God was stripped of its treasures and the people of the kingdom of Judah would have to do whatever Assyria told them in the years to come. For that, both Ahaz and the people of Jerusalem would someday pay a very high price.

THE PROPHET MICAH

Beware Samaria and Jerusalem!

Micah 1:1-3:12

There was another prophet, named Micah, who also lived in Jerusalem. He had a special message from God for the people living in Jerusalem and Samaria.

When Micah walked through the streets of Jerusalem, his heart broke for all the poor people. He saw them begging for food. He also saw the rich people walk right by them. These same rich people were often on their way to pray to false gods. Micah knew that God would someday judge these people.

Micah had a vision where he saw the Lord coming down from heaven and walking on the high places of the earth. Mountain ranges shone in the light. The entire sky seemed to dance. God's power and glory brightened everything it touched. What a sight!

Micah never forgot that glimpse of heaven. He warned God's people, "Be careful! The Lord is much more powerful than you think. He will not let you keep on living so selfishly." God wanted the leaders and priests to know it was their fault that the people had become so bad.

These leaders often stole money from the people. False prophets cheated the people. They said anything the people wanted to hear, then told them it was the will of God. They would do anything to become richer. This was very, very wrong.

Micah said, "These rulers will cry out to the Lord, but He will not answer them." It was a warning to anyone who leads people away from God.

22

God's Promise for the Future

Micah 4:1-7:20

Micah preached to the people about the past, present and future. In the past they had been very bad. In the present they were even worse.

When God showed Micah what was to happen in the future, Micah saw a time when there would finally be peace. Many nations would follow the Lord and there would be no more war. There would not even be soldiers training for war. Instead they would hammer their swords into plows.

God promised His people that even though they would be taken away as slaves, He would one day allow them to come home. At that time they would rebuild Jerusalem and their temple.

Micah also saw the time when a King would be born in Bethlehem. This was Jesus. Micah knew, even years and years before Jesus' birth that Jesus would be great, "to the ends of the earth. And this One will be our peace."

Micah said, "Listen! Someday God's people will live in safety. He will bring us peace because people all over the world will know He is a great God.

"God wants you to be just. Love being kind. Walk humbly with God."

But it made little difference. The people ignored Micah, just as they had Isaiah, Hosea and the other prophets.

23

TIME RUNS OUT

Assyria Takes Samaria

2 Kings 17:1-41; Isaiah 8:1-22; 9:8-10:34

The invasion had finally begun. It was a time of war. And as during all times of war, people were afraid. They did not know where to turn. They did not know what would happen next.

"Who will help us?" the people of Israel cried out.

They asked the question, but were not willing to act on the answer. Even though God had sent prophet after prophet to warn the people against worshiping other gods, they had not listened. They even ignored the great prophet Isaiah. He had warned of a time when they would all be made prisoner and sent away from their homes, if they did not stop being bad. But the people did not listen. Now they had brought punishment upon themselves.

For years the Assyrians had been attacking Israel, but when Hoshea became king of Israel, the Assyrians were at their strongest. Hoshea was the last king of Israel.

He was a bad king, leading the people away from God. He made a deal with the king of Assyria, trying to keep him from capturing all of Israel by paying him money. But Hoshea also made a deal with the pharaoh of Egypt, behind the back of the Assyrian king.

The Assyrian king found out about the secret deal and was not very happy. He attacked Israel and surrounded the main city, Samaria. For three years the Assyrians kept food and water from going in and out of the city.

Finally Israel surrendered. The Assyrians took all the leaders and rich people prisoner. The poor people were left behind to take care of the crops. Samaria lay in ruins. Buildings and walls had been battered into so many heaps of rubble. The people were starving from so many years of war. The Assyrians carried their prisoners off to eastern countries far, far away. "Help us!" the people cried. But it was too late.

Good King Hezekiah of Judah

2 Kings 18:1-12; 2 Chronicles 29:1-31:21

Although Assyria had made slaves out of Israel's rich and proud people, the tribe of Judah was not captured. The king of Judah at that time was a man named Hezekiah. He was a good king, the best Judah ever had.

He taught the people to follow God. Hezekiah tore down all the places on hills where other gods were worshiped. He trusted God and often asked Him to help Him lead the people.

Hezekiah also reopened the temple of God. He repaired the damage done by bad kings, including his own father. Hezekiah again made the temple into a place where people could come and pray.

"My people!" Hezekiah called out. "Now is the time to say you're sorry to God and promise to start over!"

The people of Judah listened to their king and the temple was used to offer sacrifices to God. Holy days were special again. The priests sang and played beautiful music for God as the people worshiped Him. As Hezekiah prayed for the people, the Lord forgave and healed them.

For the first time ever, all the people of Judah celebrated Passover. It was a sign of God's blessing that there was such a good harvest. They gave back to God parts of all the crops they raised. There was more than enough food for the priests. Hezekiah wanted with all his heart to please God. He relied on the Lord and loved Him more than any riches or power. Because of this, God took care of the people while Hezekiah was their king.

Hezekiah's Illness

2 Kings 20:1-20; 2 Chronicles 32:24-31; Isaiah 37:31-32; 38:1-39:8

Some years later, King Hezekiah became very, very sick. Everyone thought he would soon die. When Isaiah heard that the king was sick, he went to him.

He told the king, "The Lord has told me that you could very well die from this illness."

This upset the king very much. He cried out, "Lord! I beg You to remember how I have tried to always do what You wanted."

The Lord heard Hezekiah and spoke through Isaiah. "Hezekiah, I have heard your prayers and seen your tears. I will heal you. I will add fifteen years to your life."

Then Isaiah ordered that a cake of figs be put on Hezekiah's sores. The king's servant rushed to obey. In no time at all, the fig cake had healed Hezekiah's red sores.

When he was better, the king asked Isaiah how he could know for sure that he would really live another fifteen years. Isaiah called on God to do a miracle. The Lord made the shadow on a sundial go backwards, instead of forward!

Even though Hezekiah knew for sure that God had healed him, he did not thank God. Before his illness, Hezekiah had trusted and thanked God for everything. Afterwards he often pointed at things he had done, like building a great canal which brought water inside the city. He became proud of himself.

After his illness, Hezekiah also became proud of how rich he was and how many animals and how much land he had. A certain prince had heard that Hezekiah had been sick and came to visit. This prince came from Babylon, a small country south of Assyria. The king showed him everything in the kingdom. The prince asked the king of Judah questions about his treasure and how big his palace was and about all his riches.

After the prince left, Isaiah visited the king, asking what the prince had wanted to know. Then God gave Isaiah a look into the future. He said, "A time will come when the little country of Babylon where that prince came from, will become so great, its armies will invade Jerusalem and take away all the people here. Only a few will return. But with these few, God will rebuild Jerusalem and build up His people again."

It was a promise to remember and hold onto in the years to come.

The Assyrians Insult God

2 Kings 18:13-37; 2 Chronicles 32:7-19; Isaiah 36:1-22

Eight years after the king of Assyria captured Israel, he invaded Judah. Good King Hezekiah knew he and his people were in great danger. But he also knew if they prayed and obeyed God, He could save them.

The Assyrians surrounded a town very close to Jerusalem. Then the Assyrian king sent his generals to Hezekiah with a terrible message.

These men stood on the city walls and made fun of the Lord. They spoke loudly, using the language the people could understand. "You're going to die!" they called out. "All you people are fools if you believe Hezekiah when he tells you we Assyrians will lose! Ha! Why, we've never lost yet! Come over to our side, why don't you!"

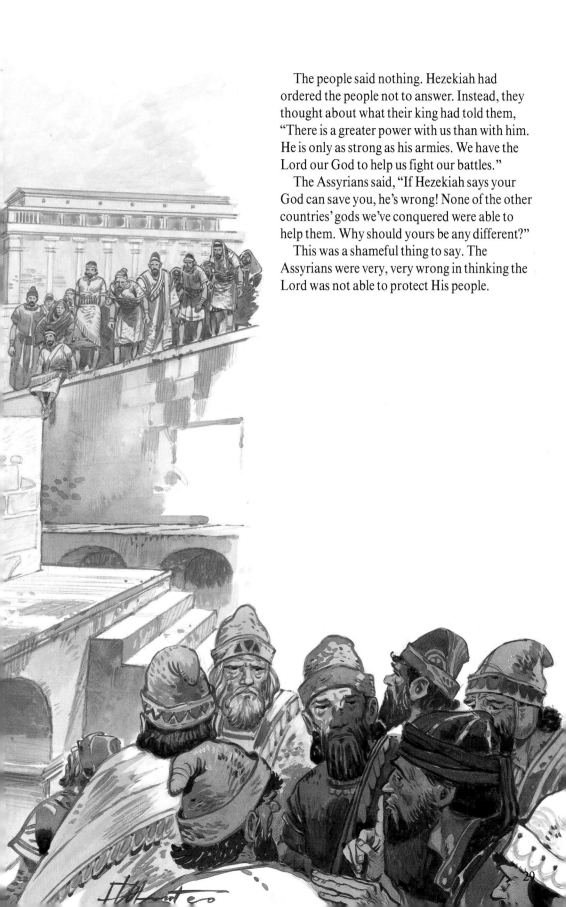

The people said nothing. Hezekiah had ordered the people not to answer. Instead, they thought about what their king had told them, "There is a greater power with us than with him. He is only as strong as his armies. We have the Lord our God to help us fight our battles."

The Assyrians said, "If Hezekiah says your God can save you, he's wrong! None of the other countries' gods we've conquered were able to help them. Why should yours be any different?"

This was a shameful thing to say. The Assyrians were very, very wrong in thinking the Lord was not able to protect His people.

Hezekiah's Prayer Saves Jerusalem

2 Kings 19:1-37; 2 Chronicles 32:20-23; Isaiah 37:1-38; Psalm 46

When Hezekiah heard how the Assyrian generals had insulted God, he could not believe his ears. He tore at his clothes, he was so upset. Hezekiah went straight to the temple and prayed to God.

While he was praying, Hezekiah's servants went to Isaiah to ask his advice. Isaiah told them, "The Lord says to tell the king not to be afraid of the Assyrians' words. God will make the Assyrian king go back to his home, and there he will die."

A little while later the king of Assyria sent Hezekiah another threatening message. Again he made fun of God. Hezekiah took the letter to the temple. Once again, he prayed, "Oh Lord, You alone are ruler of all the kingdoms of the earth. You made heaven and earth. Listen now, I pray. Listen and hear. See what the kings of Assyria have done. Save us please, Lord, so all the kingdoms may know that You alone are God."

Isaiah sent God's answer to Hezekiah. "God says, 'Because you have prayed to Me about this, I have heard you. I will protect the people. The Assyrians think they can do anything. They have become too proud. I will strike them down and make sure they do not enter Jerusalem.'"

That very night, God killed thousands and thousands of Assyrians as they camped outside Jerusalem. When their bodies were found, the rest of the army turned around and went home. Even the king of Assyria had no choice but to go home. There he died, just as Isaiah had predicted. And the people of Judah were saved.

There is a beautiful song of thanks which may have been written after this happened. It is about how God saved the people of Jerusalem. It says, "God does not want us to try to be strong on our own. Instead, we should rely on Him. Every nation should honor and obey the Lord God Almighty!"

Old Testament:

New Testament: